Second Grade Amber Brown

PAULA DANZIGER

Illustrated by Tony Ross

SCHOLASTIC INC.

New York   Toronto   London   Auckland   Sydney
Mexico City   New Delhi   Hong Kong   Buenos Aires

ISBN 0-439-79983-X

12 11 10 9 8 7 6 5 4 3 2 1   5 6 7 8 9 10/0

Printed in the U.S.A.   23

First Scholastic printing, October 2005

Designed by Gunta Alexander. Text set in Calisto.

To Sheryl Hardin,

a valuable resource (and friend) for me

and a guiding light for her students.

This second-grade teacher rules! —P. D.

It is a great second-grade day.

When I get to school,

Ms. Light beams at me.

She says that my math work is getting better.

She helps me fix Bear Lee, my backpack.

Bear Lee loves second grade.

So do I.

I am so happy. Today is a great day.

My parents didn't yell

at each other this morning.

They've been doing that a lot lately, yelling.

It is my turn to read in the tree house.

I hope this is a great day forever.

"Bright Lights!" Ms. Light claps her hands.

"Everyone, back to your desks."

I put a bookmark in the book

to remind me where I am.

Today is pocket day.

We count how many pockets we each have.

I, Amber Brown, remembered.

And I am ready.

My blue overalls have seven pockets.

I show everyone my surprise.

I am wearing my red overalls

with six pockets under my blue ones.

That's thirteen pockets!

I am pocket queen.

I get to wear the crown all day.

"Second grade rules," I say,

sitting down next to my best friend, Justin.

I think about that.

Second grade does rule.

It is the best.

And today, I am the queen.

Next is gym time.

Hannah Burton tries to trip me.

I win the race anyway.

Our gym teacher, Ms. Van Winkle,

reminds Hannah about the rule against tripping.

Next is snack time.

Ms. Light gives us snacks. Yum.

I look around the room.

Ms. Light makes it look so magical.

Ms. Light does have some rules.

Always be respectful.

Be on time.

Do your own work.

Never say "I can't."

Always say "I'll try."

I, Amber Brown, can deal with those rules.
I am not having any trouble
with second grade.
What can go wrong? And then it happens.
It is terrible. It is awful.

Ms. Light says,

"Class, I am adding a new rule today.

We have to keep our desks clean.

Some of you are getting out of control."

Ms. Light looks at me when she says that.

I, Amber Brown,

am in trouble . . . big trouble.

I can't keep a neat desk. I can't.

I know that I should say,

"I'll try," but I can't.

This rule is too hard for me.

Ms. Light says, "I just want you to know
that the desk fairy will be coming
to our room every once in a while.
She will leave treats
and a Clean Desk Award—a shiny blue ribbon—
on all the neat desks."

Tiffany Shroeder takes her thumb
out of her mouth.
She says, "I never heard of the desk fairy."
Ms. Light acts shocked.
"You've never heard of the desk fairy?"
Tiffany shakes her head.
She puts her thumb back in her mouth.

"That's okay." Ms. Light smiles.

"Her name is Deskarina.

She's a cousin of the tooth fairy."

Naomi Schwartz raises her hand.

"I have a cousin called Cindy," she says.

Everyone starts yelling out

the names of their cousins.

Ms. Light says,

"Listen to the story, class.

Deskarina's cousin, Dentalina, already

had the tooth fairy job.

Deskarina was jealous of Dentalina.

She heard about the desk fairy job.

She tried out for it . . . and she got the job."

"Wow! I never knew the tooth fairy

had a name." Naomi giggles.

"Everyone knows that," Hannah Burton says.

"But I would rather be a desk fairy

and look in desks

than be a tooth fairy and look in mouths . . .

and touch other people's dirty teeth.

That would be disgusting."

"My dad is a dentist," Fredrich says,

taking his finger out of his nose.

"It is good to touch other people's teeth."

I hope that Fredrich's father

is not a nose-picker like his son.

A nose-picking dentist . . . yuck.

Ms. Light says, "Use your imaginations
to write about and draw Deskarina."
I love doing this.
But a clean desk?
I don't know if I can do that.
I think about it . . . a Clean Desk Award.
I want one.
I write about Deskarina.
Then I draw her.
She is wearing a purple dress and purple shoes.
She is wearing desk jewelry.
Her hair is pink, with glitter stars in it.
She's carrying a large backpack.
It's filled with treats and awards
for boys and girls with clean desks.

She also has notes in the backpack.

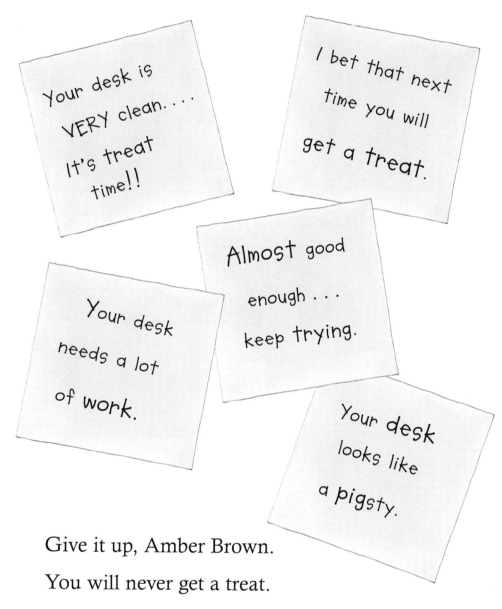

Your desk is VERY clean. . . . It's treat time!!

I bet that next time you will get a treat.

Almost good enough . . . keep trying.

Your desk needs a lot of work.

Your desk looks like a pigsty.

Give it up, Amber Brown.

You will never get a treat.

Your desk should be named a disaster zone.

I draw the Deskmobile.

Deskarina will drive it all over the world,

checking on desks.

It is much nicer than the tooth fairy's vehicle,

the Molar Express.

Lunch is next. Justin and I share.

We dunk my potato chips into his pudding.

I eat half of his peanut butter

and banana sandwich.

He eats half of my tuna fish sandwich.

He asks,

"If a rooster lays an egg on a slanted roof,

will it roll to the left or the right?"

I think about it. I don't know.

Justin laughs and yells, "Neither.

Roosters don't lay eggs. Chickens do."

Justin flaps his arms like a chicken
and makes chicken sounds.
Justin has decided that second grade
is the year of the chicken joke.
He is even thinking about
starting a chicken club.

It is time to go back to class.

I keep thinking about my desk.

How come some people have

no problem keeping their desks clean?

How come I can't?

I look in my desk.

It is filled with a lot of stuff.

I don't have time to clean it out.

Justin's mom is picking us up.

For the rest of the week,

I throw out one thing every day.

But, somehow, I put two more things in.

Deskarina does not come this week.

Next week, there is still no desk fairy.

I give up cleaning my desk.

If the fairy has trouble finding our school,

why should I bother?

And then it happens.

We all come into class.

There are ribbons and treats

on some desks.

Hannah Burton has them.

She acts so proud.

No one else in our group got any . . .

not Justin, not me, not Fredrich.

I look in my desk.

I see what Deskarina found . . .

five almost-empty potato chip wrappers,

a broken shoelace, seven library books,

a letter I was writing to Aunt Pam,

a crumpled page of my book report,

and six malted milk balls covered with lint.

I guess Deskarina didn't think

my desk was clean enough.

I go home and tell my mom.

Mom tells me to practice on my room.

She says it would be a treat . . . for her . . .

if we could find my floor sometimes.

I should never have told Mom

about Deskarina.

I go to my room. Cleaning is so boring.

I find my missing pink sock

with the silver glitter stars on it.

I thought that the washing machine ate it.

I empty out a dresser drawer.

I pretend it is the inside of my desk.

Pencils here. Pens there.

Extra scrunchies here. Books there.

It seems easy. I will do it at school.

I get to school.

Everyone is standing around Bobby's desk.

He has brought his pet iguana, Ike, to school.

I have to make a decision . . .

meet Ike or clean my desk.

I meet Ike.

Two days later, Deskarina visits again.

My desk is still messy.

This time Justin and Fredrich

and Hannah Burton get treats from Deskarina.

I am so unhappy. No ribbon for me.

Justin shares his treat with me.

But it is not the same as getting my own.

I, Amber Brown,

am beginning to dislike Deskarina.

Ms. Light says not to worry.

She sees improvement.

If I work a little harder,

she thinks Deskarina will see it, too.

I clean my desk during free time.

I put everything that I need in my backpack.

For three days, I do not touch my desk.

I use my backpack.

Ms. Light says that I cannot do that.

I, Amber Brown,

am beginning to dislike rules.

But, I, Amber Brown,

really want a Clean Desk Award.

I can spell.

Why can't I keep my desk clean?

Even math is easier than keeping my desk clean.

I keep trying.

Finally, I figure it out.

Instead of stuffing garbage in my desk,

I walk to the trash can.

It is boring to throw things out.

It is easier to just put them in my desk.

But I keep working at it.

Finally, my desk is clean.

Deskarina has not come back.

This time, I keep my desk clean.

It's amazing.

It is so much easier to find things.

Today, Justin and I are late.

My dad's car got a flat tire.

Class has already started.

We rush in.

People clap. Even Ms. Light claps.

Tiffani points to my desk.

Deskarina was here last night.

She left me a treat . . .

and a ribbon.

I, Amber Brown,

have a Clean Desk Award!

I am so happy. I wear my ribbon.

I share my treat with Justin.

He didn't get one this time.

Then I throw the used paper

in the trash can instead of in my desk.

Tonight I will put the ribbon

on my bulletin board in my room . . .

as soon as I find a place for it.